FIRST IMPRESSIONS
An Intermediate Piano Method

Mid Intermediate Theory • VOLUME 2

MUSIC THEORY

M'lou Dietzer

(800) 876-9777
10075 SW Beav-Hills Hwy (503) 641-5691
1010 SE Powell (503) 775-0800
12334 SE Division (503) 760-6881

*Music theory correlating with the
Music and Study Guide Series including
worksheets, musical experiments, ear training,
sight reading, projects and quizzes*

Copyright © MCMXCIX by Alfred Publishing Co., Inc.
All rights reserved. Printed in the USA.
ISBN 0-7390-0733-5

Cover art: Yellow, Red, Blue, *1925
by Vasily Kandinsky (Russian, 1866–1944)
Oil on canvas, 127 x 200 cm
Collections du Centre Georges Pompidou
Musée national d'art moderne, Paris*

THEORY SERIES

TABLE OF CONTENTS

First Impressions Theory Series
Mid Intermediate • Volume 2

Chapter 1
Rhythm: Meter; Rhythmic Motive 3

Chapter 2
Major Scales: Keys of Four Sharps and Keys of Four Flats; Tonic and Dominant; Cycle of Fifths 9

Chapter 3
Minor Scales: Parallel Minor 15

Chapter 4
Intervals: Inversions 21

Chapter 5
Chords: V^7 27

Chapter 6
Phrases and Period; Nonharmonic Tones; Dissonance/Resolution 33

Glossary 37

Quiz 38

Sight reading 40

NOTE TO THE TEACHER

This theory book is organized into chapters, each of which can be covered in four to six weeks. It is best to present the chapters and material in them in the order written, as each element leads to the next.

The following sections in each chapter can be assigned as homework and checked at the lesson:

Musical experiment

Worksheet

Quiz

Sight reading

Project

A few highlights in Volume 2:

Chapter 2: Learning how to transpose (p. 14).

Chapter 6: Learning to identify nonharmonic tones in music (p. 34–35).

At the end of the book: A page of signs and terms plus a quiz and sightreading.

Ear training in each chapter.

In the *First Impressions Theory Series*, the learning technique of spiraling is applied—that is, material is continuously reviewed and reinforced before new material is presented. This series is written to ensure thorough understanding at each step of learning and prepares the student for more complex topics in advanced levels.

All musical examples in this book are taken from Volume 2 of the *First Impressions Music and Study Guide Series*; each example has a page reference. The teacher can play examples that are too hard for the student to sight read. The student should hear and learn to play all of the examples. As much as possible, the topics in the *Theory Series* correlate with the *Music and Study Guide Series*. The remaining volumes in the *Theory Series* expand old concepts and add new ones, providing an understanding of the wonderful world of intermediate piano literature. Together, the two series facilitate the transition into advanced theory and repertoire.

Abbreviations used in this book:

RH, LH = *right hand, left hand*
HT, HS = *hands together, hands separately.*

CHAPTER 1

Rhythm: Meter; Rhythmic Motive

Review of C and ₵

In some pieces, **C** is used as the time signature instead of 4/4.

It is often called *common time* since 4/4 is used in many pieces.

The **₵** is used to represent 2/2.

It is often called *cut time* since the vertical line "cuts" both of the 4s in 4/4 time in half.

In **₵**, what kind of note would get one count: *quarter note* ___ *half note* ___?

March, from Anna Magdalena Bach's Notebook, *meas. 1–3, p. 6*

Meter

METER means *to measure*.
The time signature tells the meter of each piece.
Below are some time signatures presented in previous volumes:

$$\frac{3}{4} \quad \frac{4}{8} \quad \frac{2}{4} \quad \frac{3}{8} \quad \frac{4}{4} \quad \frac{2}{2}$$

A time signature can be described as:

3/4 shows that there are three quarter notes in each measure.

4/8 shows that there are four eighth notes in each measure.

Another way to describe a time signature is:

The top number tells you how many beats are in each measure.

The bottom number tells you what kind of a note gets one beat.

Another way to express meter

If the time signature is 2/4 or 2/2, there are two beats in each measure.
 Another way to express this is: 2/4 is **duple meter,** and 2/2 is **duple meter.**
If the time signature is 4/4 or 4/8, there are four beats in each measure.
 Another way to express this is: 4/4 is **quadruple meter,** and 4/8 is **quadruple meter.**
3/4 or 3/8 have three beats in the measure;

 do these time signatures show ___duple ___or triple meter?

In 6/8, the eighth notes are called "small beats" and the dotted quarters or their equivalent are called "big beats".

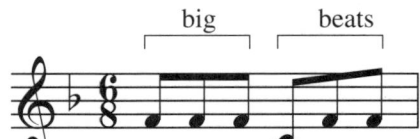

two big beats in each measure

Review: there are two groups of small beats in each measure of the *Irish Washer Woman:* the two big beats are sensed more strongly than the individual small beats. Therefore, the two big beats make 6/8 a **duple meter.**

Worksheet

Draw lines to match each time signature with the appropriate description.

- three eighth notes in each measure •
- two half notes in each measure •
- three quarter notes in each measure •
- four quarter notes in each measure •

- • 3/4
- • 4/4
- • 2/2
- • 3/8

Write the time signature for this example:

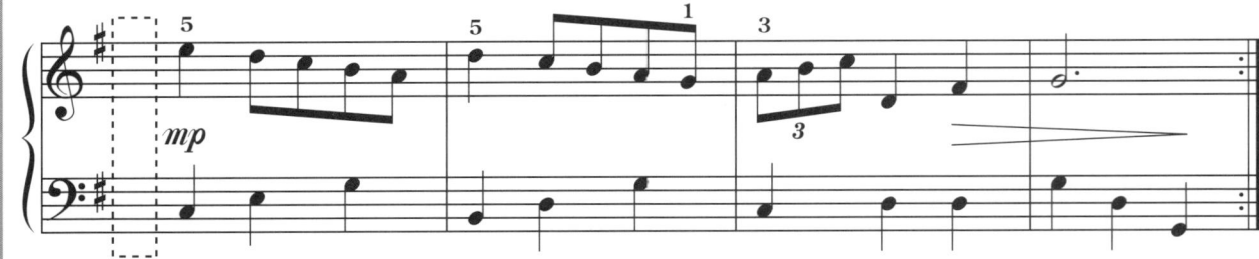

Minuet, from Anna Magdalena Bach's Notebook, meas. 13–16, p. 4

Draw lines to match each time signature with the appropriate meter.

Two of the time signatures are duple meter.

- duple meter •
- triple meter •
- duple meter •
- quadruple meter •

- • 4/8
- • 2/4
- • 3/4
- • 6/8

Review: groups of three eighth notes and groups of two eighth notes in the same piece

In the example below, quarter beats are divided into groups of three eighths to form triplets and groups of two eighths in the natural division. Tap the rhythm:

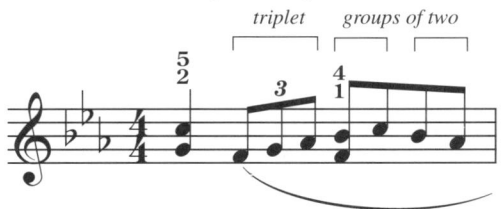

Pease Summer Musings, RH, meas. 3, Volume 1, p. 21.

16th notes and triplet eighth notes in the same piece

Use a metronome and tap the rhythm of the following example.

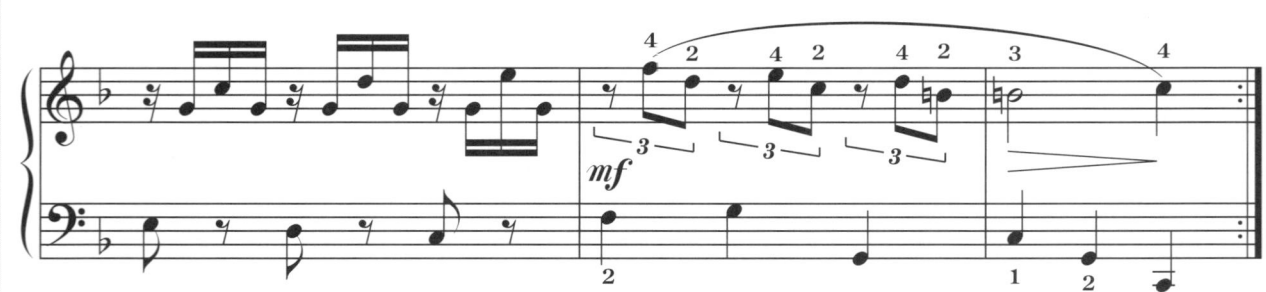

Mozart Minuet, meas. 8–10, p. 8

Rhythmic groups divided between the hands

In Mozart's *Minuet,* notes are divided between the hands:

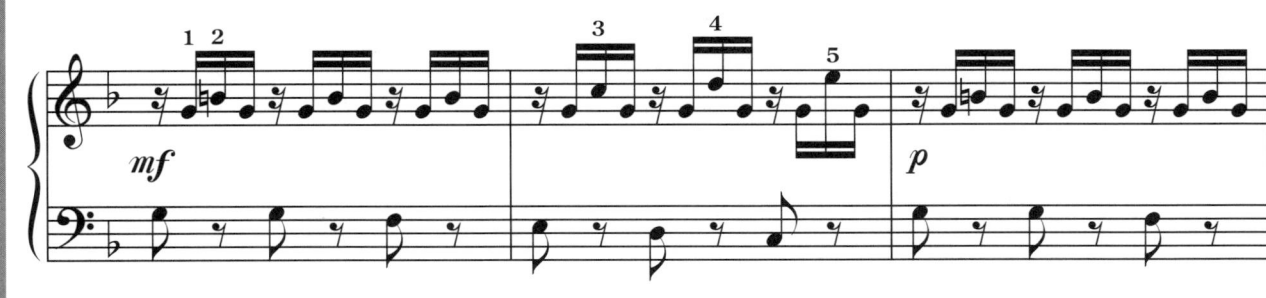

Mozart Minuet, *meas. 5–7, p. 8*

In the above example, what note occurs in the LH? *16th note* ___ *eighth note* ___

What rest occurs in the RH? *16th rest* ___ *eighth rest* ___

Tap each of the following; do they both sound the same? *yes* ___ *no* ___

A.

B.

Rhythmic motive

A **motive** is a small unit of music used often throughout a composition. In Rebikov's *The Clown,* a rhythmic motive of two 16th notes and one eighth note is seen in RH, meas. 2:

Rebikov The Clown, *RH, meas. 2, p. 18*

In RH, meas. 13–16, the rhythmic motive occurs in sequences:

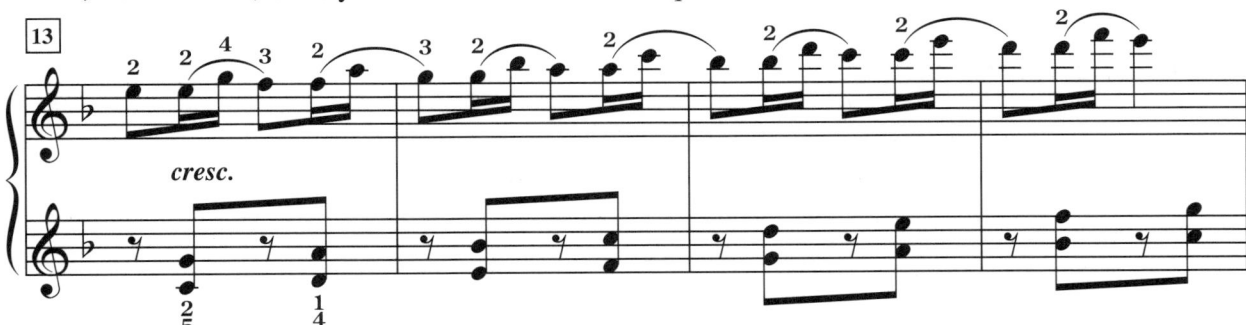

meas. 13–16

In meas. 2, the interval between the two 16ths is a third ___ *second* ___.
In meas. 13–16, the interval between the two 16ths is a third ___ *second* ___.

• In meas. 13–16, the pitch in the motive is changed but the rhythm is unchanged.

Another rhythmic motive is seen in meas. 1–2 of Spindler's *Sonatina* Op. 157, No. 4, second movement:

This is the same rhythm notes of ♫♩ seen in Rebikov's *The Clown.*
• In *The Clown,* the motive starts on the "and" of a beat and sounds better if the LAST note of the motive is stressed.

meas. 1–2

• In *Sonatina,* the motive starts ON the beat and sounds better if the FIRST note of each motive is stressed.

Upbeats and downbeats

Upbeats can occur before the first beat of a measure as well as before other beats in the measure. In meas. 2 of the previous Rebikov example, the set of two 16ths in the motive are upbeats to beat two.

In meas. 13, the first set of 16th notes comes before beat 1__ beat 2 ___ and
the second set of 16th notes comes before beat___ of the next measure.

In the following example, a quarter-note upbeat begins the piece.
At the end of meas. 1, two eighth notes are substituted for the quarter note upbeat.
In the second example, the pattern of two eighth note upbeats (circled) recur in each hand.

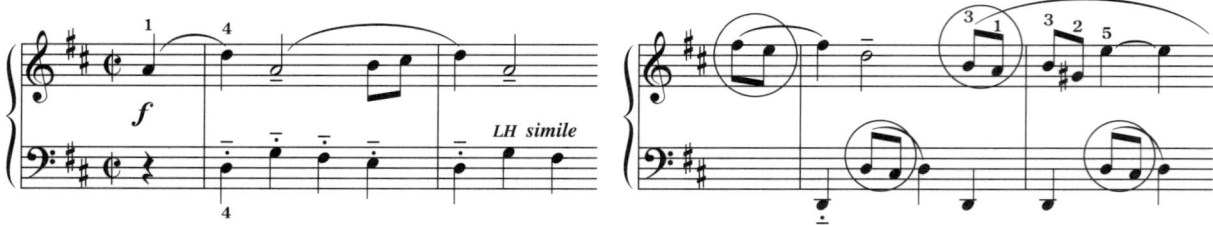

March, from Anna Magdalena Bach's Notebook,
meas. 1–2, p. 6, with upbeat

meas. 5–6, with upbeat

In meas. 5–6, the LH imitates the  pattern of the RH.
Look at the meter of 𝄵 again and then answer the following question:

The LH's two eighth notes in meas. 5–6 are upbeats to beat 2 ___ beat 3 ___ .

Grace notes

In Kullak's *Dance on the Lawn*, the grace notes are played like very quick upbeats:

Kullak Dance on the Lawn, meas. 3, p. 15

Musical experiment

With your RH, tap the following rhythm pattern. Stress the dotted eighth note and play the 16th note quickly and lightly.
You see that the dotted eighth and 16th note form a *visual unit:*

When you tap the example, you sense the
16th note as a quick upbeat to the half note.
Therefore, the 16th note and half note which follows form a *musical unit* of:

- Musically, each 16th note in the RH of the following example belongs to the longer note which follows.

Finish drawing a circle around each musical unit. Tap the example.

Kabalevsky, Sonatina in A Minor, Op. 27, No. 18, *meas. 1–4 with upbeat, p. 20*

Strong and weak beat patterns

The first beat of a measure is often (but not always) played with a slight accent.
The other beats are usually weaker beats and are played more lightly. In this example,
the LH's first beat in each measure forms a melody that blends with the RH melody.
In this case, a slight stress on the LH's first beats is appropriate.

Gurlitt Song Without Words, *meas. 1–4, p. 14*   The LH and RH melodies

This example shows a common pattern for a
single measure in duple, triple and quadruple
meter; in this pattern, the last beat is a weak beat:

Upbeats are often written on weaker beats and played softer than downbeats.

In the following example, the four sixteenths form an upbeat pattern to the next measure.
In this case, it is appropriate to crescendo as marked, from beat 2 to beat 1 of the measure:

Spindler Sonatina, Op. 157, No. 4, *2nd movt., RH, meas. 54–57, p. 13*

Syncopation

Syncopation is an accent on what is usually a weak beat of the measure.
In the example below, how else could the time signature be written? 4/4 ___ 2/4 ___ 2/2 ___

How many beats are in each measure? *four* ___ *two* ___

On what beat of the measure does the RH half note occur? *beat 2* ___ *the & of 1* ___

March, from Anna Magdalena Bach's Notebook,
meas. 1–2, with upbeat, p.6

- Each RH half note is an example of syncopation.

Ear training

Mark an X on the answer line next to the example your teacher taps.

Teacher: *Choose one of each set to tap.*

1.

2.

Sight reading

Tap both parts of each example hands together, or tap the examples like a duet with your teacher.

1.
2.

Quiz

1. The LH in this example shows

   *downbeats*____
   *syncopation*____

Kabalevsky Sonatina in A Minor, Op. 27, No. 18, *meas. 1–2, p. 20*

2. *On what beats of the measure are the two eighth-note upbeats written?*_____

Kullak Dance on the Lawn, *meas. 1 with upbeat, p. 15*

3. Write in the counts:

4. What is the meter of $\frac{6}{8}$? *duple* ___ *triple*____

Project: creating rhythm patterns

Combine any two of the following boxes to form a longer rhythmic pattern.

   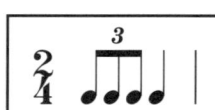

Write your pattern here and then, tap it:

Write a contrasting pattern in the second measure to complete a two-measure pattern, then tap it.

CHAPTER 2

Major Scales: Keys of Four Sharps and Keys of Four Flats; Tonic and Dominant; Cycle of Fifths

Major scales

Review: A tetrachord is the pattern of whole-whole-half step.

Major scales are created by playing two tetrachords separated by a whole step.

A major scale shares each of its tetrachords with a scale above and a scale below.

The half step and tetrachords are marked with a ∧ and ⌐ ⌐.

Play each scale below using LH fingers 5–4–3–2 and RH fingers 2–3–4–5 for tetrachords.

The F, C and G major scales:

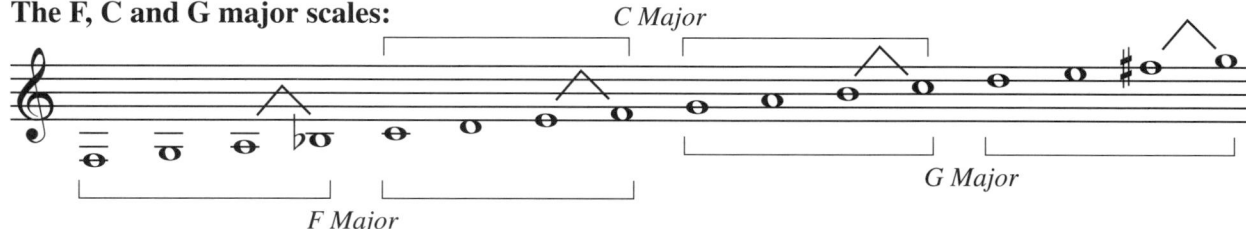

In addition to these three scales, you have learned D, A, B♭ and E♭ major scales.

Their key signatures are written; practice copying each one:

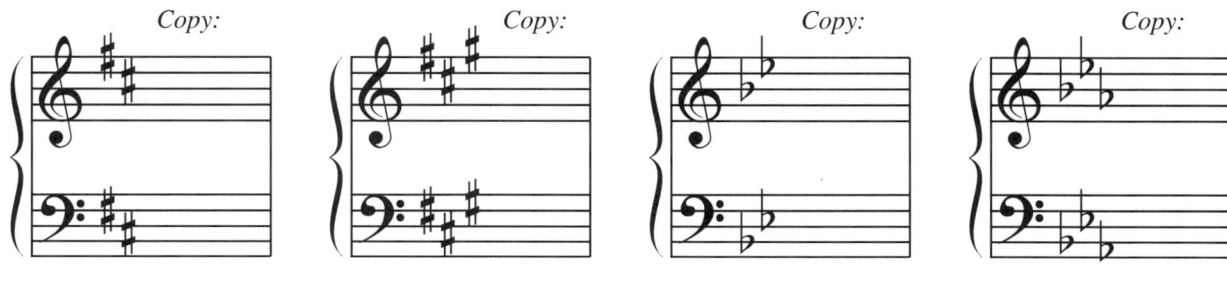

Write the two tetrachords of the A major scale.

Mark half steps with a ∧ and tetrachords with a ⌐ ⌐.

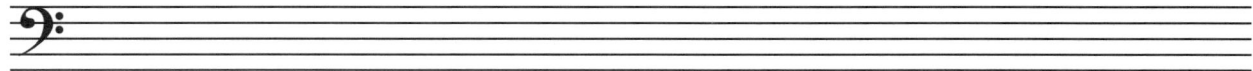

Play the upper tetrachord of A major with your LH.

With your RH, start on A_____ B_____ and play another tetrachord, creating a new major scale.

The name of the new scale is ____ major and it has three___ four ___ sharps.

Write your new scale here, placing the sharp symbols before the appropriate notes.

The key signature for this new scale is shown; practice copying the key signature.

When you write sharps or flats, be sure the line or space shows in the open part of the symbol:

Now, write the two tetrachords of the E♭ major scale;
mark half steps with a ∧ and tetrachords with a ⌐────────⌐.

Play the lower tetrachord of E♭ major with your RH. *Name the RH's top note: ____ .*

One octave below the RH's top note, place LH's fifth finger and build a new tetrachord.
- Do the top and bottom notes of major scales always have the same letter name? yes ___ no___

   The name of your new scale is ___ major and it has three___ four ___ flats.

Write your new scale below, placing the flat symbols before the appropriate notes.

Copy:

The key signature for this new scale is shown;
practice copying the key signature:

New names for some scale degrees

The first scale degree is called the **tonic note**.
"Tonic" comes from the Greek word *tonikos* that means "capable of extension."
Tetrachords begin on a given note to create a major scale. The first scale degree,
therefore, is "capable of extension" into a scale pattern.

The fifth scale degree is called the **dominant note**.
The word "dominant" means "most prominent" or
"important in position." One reason it is a very
important note: the upper tetrachord of a major scale
begins on the dominant note.

The fourth scale degree is called the **subdominant.**
The prefix "sub" means "under" or "below."
The word "subdominant" names the scale degree
that is a perfect fifth *below* the tonic:

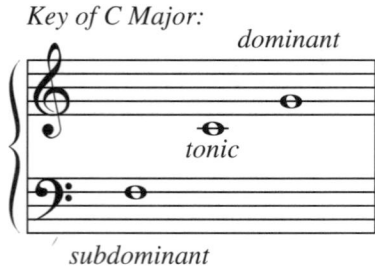

Look at the first music example on the previous page to review how
the three scales of F, C and G overlap.
F is the subdominant of C and G is the dominant of C.
- All major scales overlap with a scale above and a scale below.

Gathering the major scales together on the cycle of fifths

Preliminary: The tonic notes of all the scales presented so far are shown below.
Play all of the tonics in sets of two (such as A♭ and E♭, E♭ and B♭, etc.)
to see that each interval between adjacent tonics is a

perfect fourth ___ *perfect fifth* ___.

The names of the scales can be charted on a circle that is called the **cycle (or circle) of fifths.**
To understand one reason this diagram is called the cycle of fifths,
remember that the interval of a fifth occurs between adjacent tonics.

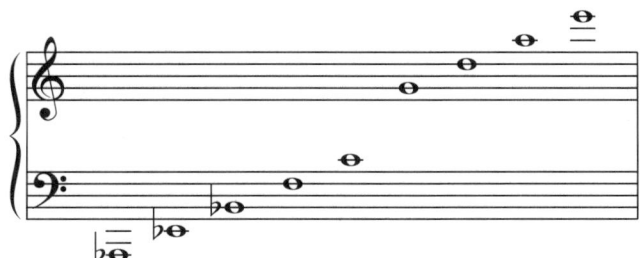
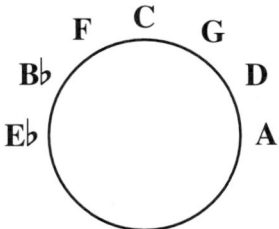

A further understanding of the cycle of fifths

The number of sharps in the cycle of fifths corresponds to the numbers on a clock.
Imagine the same numbers on the opposite side of the clock's face to remember
the number of flats in each flat key.

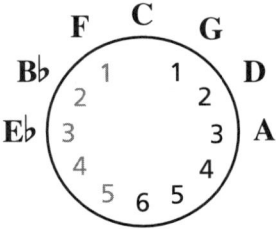

How many minutes separate the numbers on a clock? ___
How many letter names separate each of the major scales in the cycle? ___

- Because the answer to both of these questions is "5",
  the clock face is a good pattern to use for the *cycle of fifths!*

Find the specific spot on the cycle of fifths
where the E and the A♭ major scales belong.

Add these new scales of four sharps and flats
to the cycles above.

The cycle of fifths shown here is incomplete; it will be
continued in later *First Impressions* Theory Books.

Worksheet

Copy these key signatures. Identify the major key of each signature.

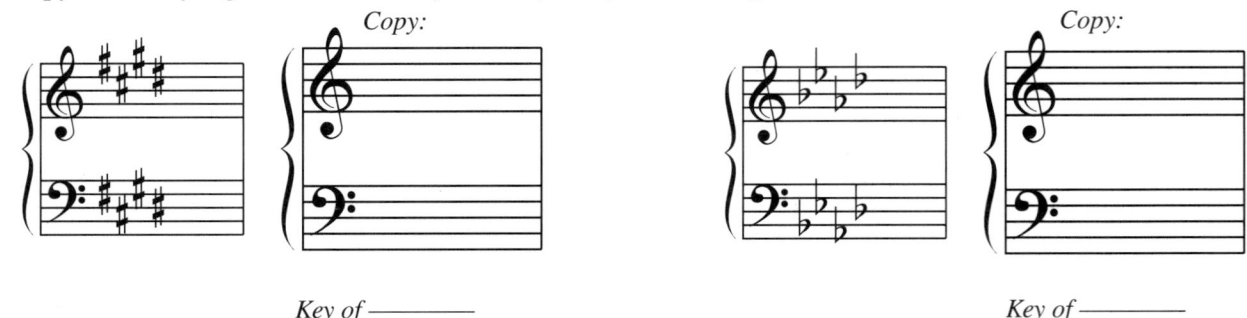

Key of _____   Key of _____

Musical experiment

Sharp key signatures always begin with F♯ and flat key signatures always begin with B♭.
Also, the sharps and flats are always in the same order no matter how many symbols there are.
Why is that?

To answer this question, finish filling in the following chart.
Always copy the sharp or sharps you wrote for the previous scale
and add the new sharp so that F♯ is always first, C♯ is always second, and so on:

The major scale with only one sharp is ____ .   *The sharp is F♯.*
The major scale with two sharps is ____ .   *The sharps are F♯ and ____ .*
The major scale with three sharps is ____ .   *The sharps are ____ , ____ and ____ .*
The major scale with four sharps is ____ .   *The sharps are ____ , ____ , ____ and ____ .*

Look at the key signature for E major in the worksheet above; are sharps in the
signature in the order you wrote for the major scale with four sharps?

yes____ no____

From doing this experiment, you can understand why the flats in key signatures
also follow a certain order. Finish writing the order of flats in the A♭ major key signature
by building scales in the descending order of F, B♭, E♭ and A♭ major: ___ ___ ___ ___

Ear training

Your teacher will play each scale, but will omit one note in each scale.
Circle the omitted notes.

Teacher: *Play each scale, omitting one note in each scale.*

Sight reading

1. On the keyboard, locate all the flats used in this piece.
2. Study all fingering; it is designed to help you learn the B♭ major scale.
3. Silently practice the fingering for the RH and for the LH in meas. 6–8. Then silently practice the fingering hands together.
4. Notice that this is a slow piece.

Quiz

1. This example shows a scale passage that does not start on the tonic note.

   What major scale is used for this example? _____ *major*

   Spindler Sonatina, Op. 157, No. 4, *2nd movt., RH meas. 7–8, p. 12*

2. Name the key of this example. _____ *major*

3. Write the key signature for E major and for A♭ major:

4. Write the upper tetrachord of the E♭ major scale:

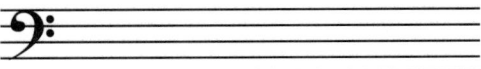

5. Write the lower tetrachord of the B♭ major scale:

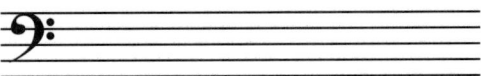

6. Are the two tetrachords you just wrote the same? *yes* ___ *no* ___

Project: *transposing*

Following is *On the Bridge at Avignon*, written in the key of F major.

The following questions will help you transpose the piece to the key of D major:

1. *On what scale degree does the piece begin in F major?* _____

2. *What note name will you use to start the song in D major?* _____

3. *Name the sharps for D major:* ____ ♯ *and* ____ ♯

First, write the key signature for D major, and then
write measures 1 and 2 of the piece. Measures 3 and 4 are already written:

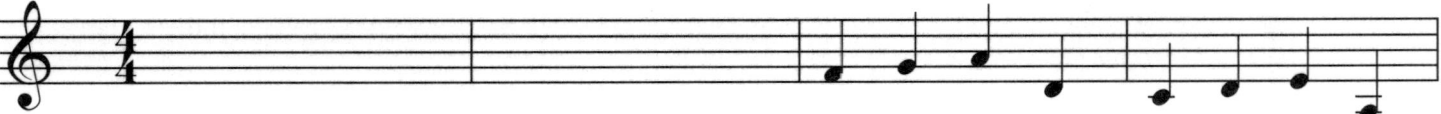

Write the next two measures, 5 and 6; the end of the song is already written:

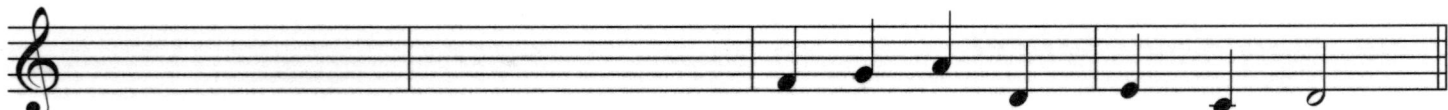

Play and sing the whole song, which is now in the key of D major.
• If you want, you can transpose the song to another key, such as G major.

CHAPTER 3
Minor Scales: Parallel Minor

Important facts about minor scales

- Minor scales are contained in major scales. Begin on degree 6 of any major scale and play the same notes used in the major scale for a full octave to hear the minor scale:

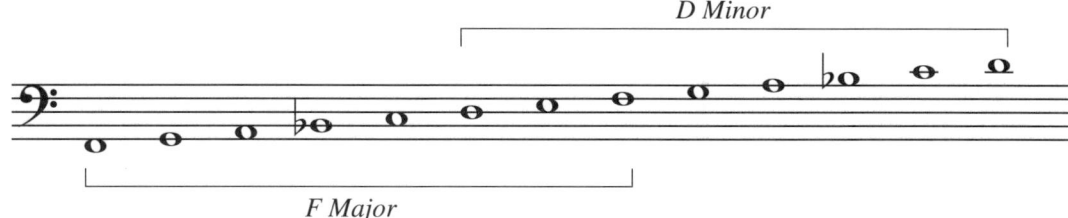

- Major and minor scales that share the same key signature are called "relatives." F major and D minor seen above are **relative major and minor scales.**

- Minor scales have three forms: natural, harmonic and melodic. The natural form uses only the notes found in its "parent" major scale:

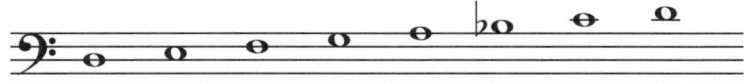

- To create the harmonic form, raise the seventh degree of any natural minor scale a half step to make a wide space between scale degrees 6 and 7 and a half step between the top two notes.

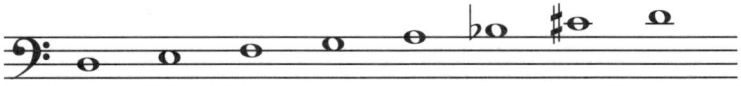

- The third form of the minor scale is the melodic form. Ascending, raise scale degrees 6 and 7 a half step; descending, lower scale degrees 6 and 7 a half step. The descending scale will be the same as the natural form.

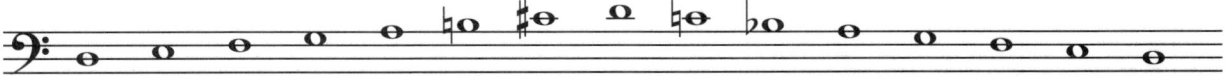

Review and worksheet

You have learned the A, D, E, G and B minor scales.

To find the relative major of any minor scale, play the first three notes of the minor scale. The third note is the tonic of the relative major scale.

Fill in the blanks with letter names:

The relative major of A minor is _____ major and it has no ♯s or ♭s in the key signature.

The relative major of G minor is _____ major and it has _____ ♭s in the signature.

The relative major of B minor is _____ major and it has _____ ♯s in the signature.

Using accidentals, write the G natural minor scale and its relative major scale:
G minor   *Relative major*

𝄢   𝄢

Using accidentals, write the B natural minor scale and its relative major scale:
B minor   *Relative major*

𝄢   𝄢

Minor scales also belong on the cycle of fifths

Each minor key is written inside the cycle of fifths, close to its relative major.
Fill in the missing relative minors of B♭ and D major; use lower case letters for minor:

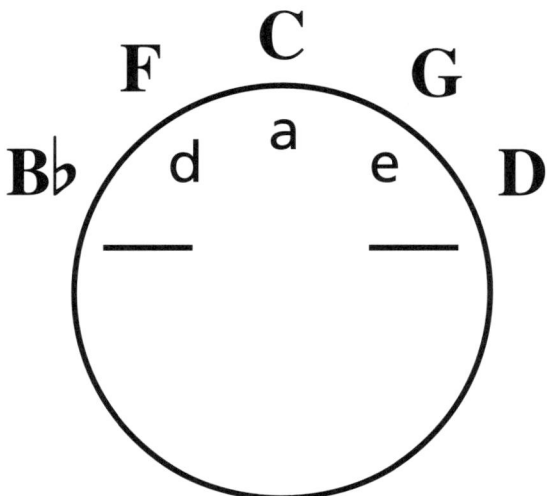

A new minor scale

Start with the C major tetrachords and play descending overlapping tetrachords until you arrive at the major scale of three flats.

Using accidentals, write the major scale of three flats below.

Circle scale degree 6 in the scale to find the name of the new minor scale.

  The name is ___ minor.

Add the major and minor keys of three flats to the cycle of fifths above.

Worksheet

Write the natural minor scale of three flats; the key signature is written.
Now, add an accidental to create the harmonic form.
Ask your teacher to write in finger numbers for each hand, and then play the scale HS.

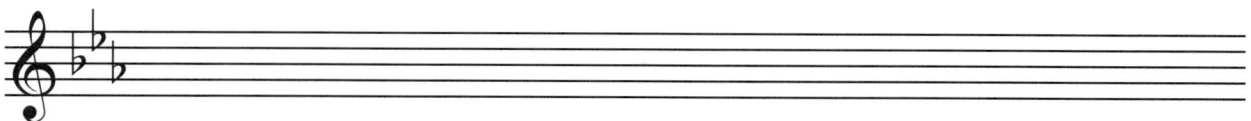

Parallel major and minor keys

Slowly play the following examples and listen for the sound of major and minor:

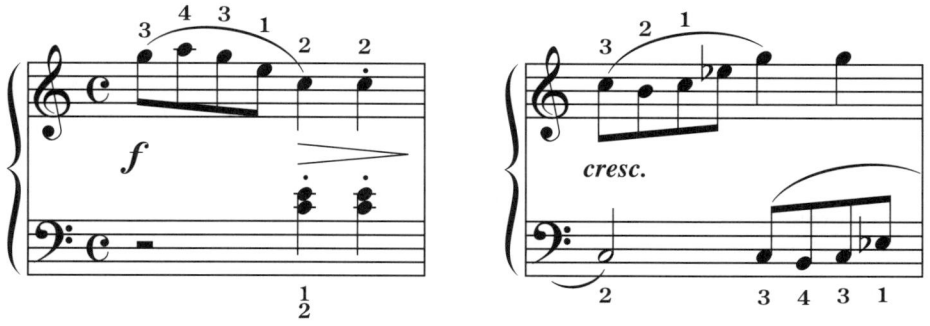

Spindler Sonatina Op. 157, No. 4, *1st movt., meas. 1 and 10*

In meas. 1, did you hear C major ___ or C minor ___ ?
In meas. 10, did you hear C major ___ or C minor ___ ?
Look at the key signature; what key has no sharps or flats? ____ major

In meas. 10, Spindler created the sound of C minor by using accidentals instead of a key signature.

- C major and C minor share the same tonic and are called **parallel major and minor keys**.

Musical experiment: determining key signatures for parallel minors

If Spindler had wanted to write a key signature for the meas. 10 example above,
how could you find out what it would be?

Write the third scale degree of C minor to determine the relative major: ____ ♭.

Write the major scale that begins on that note; use accidentals:

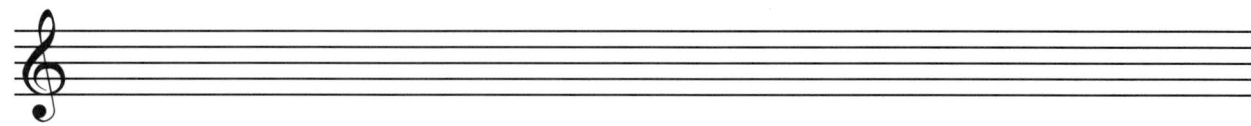

If Spindler had used a key signature for C minor,
how many flats would he have used? ____

What does it mean to play in a major or minor key?

Playing in a certain key such as G major or E minor means the composer uses notes contained in that major or minor scale. Occasionally, the composer can add accidentals for interest or to create the harmonic or melodic minor form. Play each of these examples slowly and listen for the sound of G major in meas. 1–4 and E minor in meas. 9–12:

Kullak Dance on the Lawn, *meas. 1–4, p. 15*

meas. 9–12

In meas. 1–4, Kullak used accidentals such as G♯ in meas. 1 and A♯ in meas. 2 to make a more interesting sound; basically, the key remains G major.

Write the E harmonic minor scale:

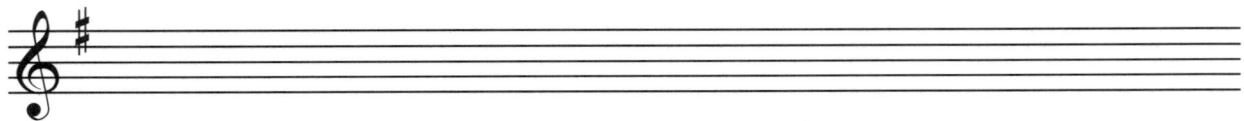

In meas. 9–10, Kullak used D♯ to create the harmonic form of the E minor scale.

In meas. 10–11, arrows mark accidentals written to create interest. The bracket shows C♮ and D♯ used to reinforce the E minor harmonic form.

Review: a sister and brother are related by having the same parents; major and minor scales are related by having the same key signature.

The relative minor of G major is _____ minor.

The relative major of E minor is _____ major.

Ear training

Your teacher will tell you the starting note and then play a minor scale in one of its forms. Identify the form, choose a clef and then write the scale.

Form: natural____ harmonic____ melodic____

Teacher: *Play an easy minor scale in melodic form, ascending and descending.*

Sight reading

As you play, watch carefully for accidentals. After you play, answer the question below.

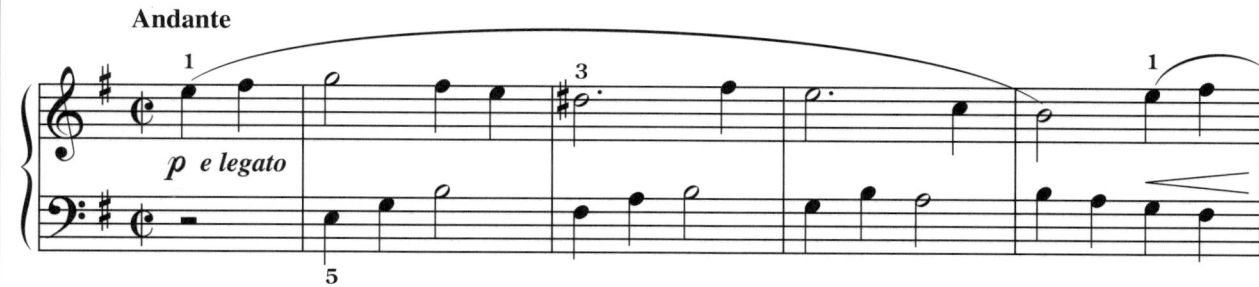

Meas. 1–4 sounded minor and meas. 5–8 sounded _____ .

Quiz

Example #1

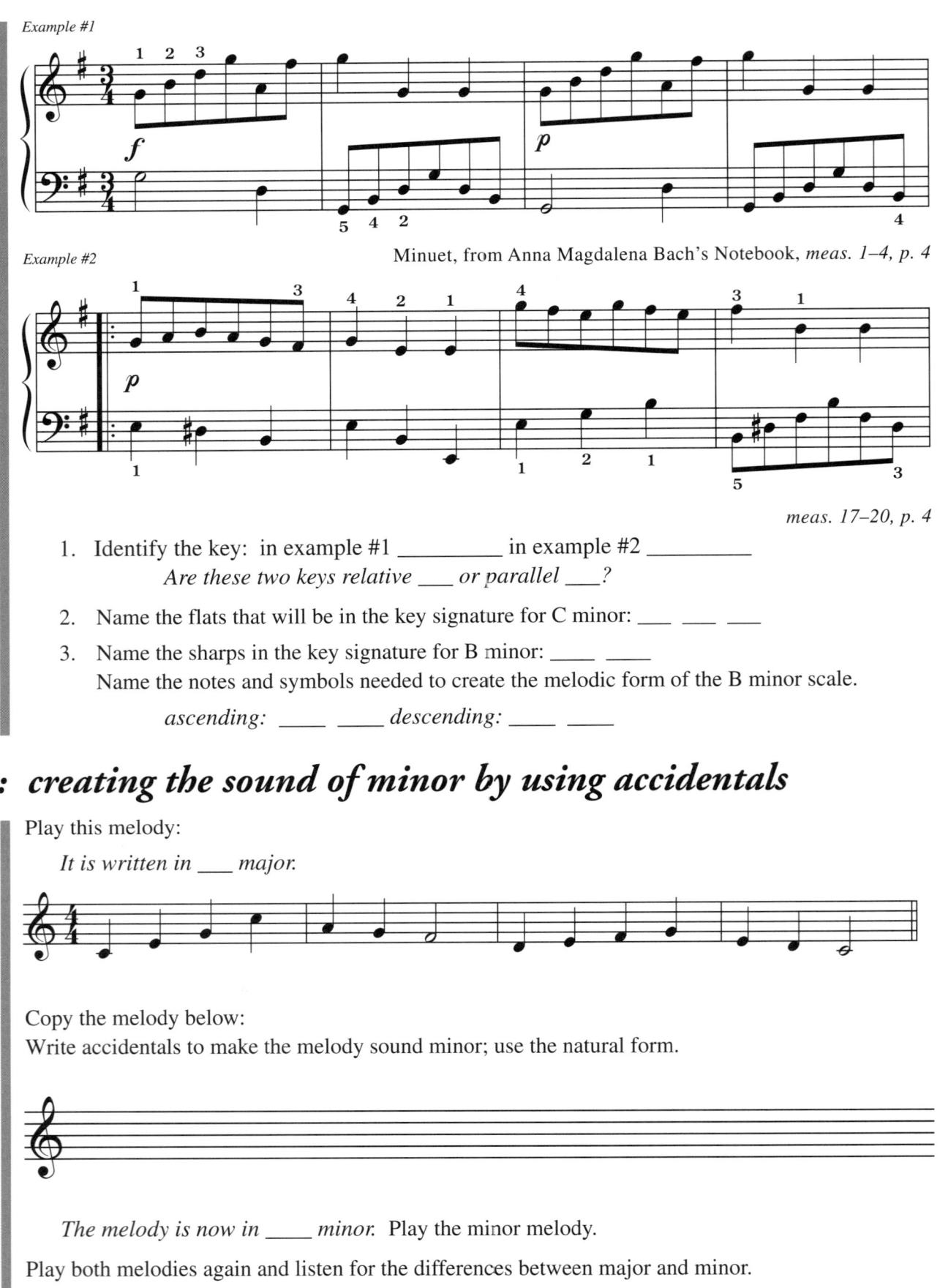

Example #2

Minuet, from Anna Magdalena Bach's Notebook, *meas. 1–4, p. 4*

meas. 17–20, p. 4

1. Identify the key: in example #1 _____ in example #2 _____
   Are these two keys relative ___ or parallel ___?

2. Name the flats that will be in the key signature for C minor: ___ ___ ___

3. Name the sharps in the key signature for B minor: ____ ____
   Name the notes and symbols needed to create the melodic form of the B minor scale.
   ascending: ____ ____ *descending:* ____ ____

Project: *creating the sound of minor by using accidentals*

Play this melody:

It is written in ___ major.

Copy the melody below:
Write accidentals to make the melody sound minor; use the natural form.

The melody is now in ____ minor. Play the minor melody.

Play both melodies again and listen for the differences between major and minor.

The two keys are: parallel____ relative____ major and minor.

CHAPTER 4
Intervals: Inversions

Review: *interval qualities*

2nds, 3rds, 6ths and 7ths can be major, minor, diminished or augmented.
4ths, 5ths and octaves (8ths) can be perfect, diminished or augmented.
Build any major scale with two tetrachords; start on the tonic and go up to each scale degree to find the major and perfect intervals.

Create the other qualities by reducing or enlarging the M and P intervals. Here is the chart on which all intervals are organized:

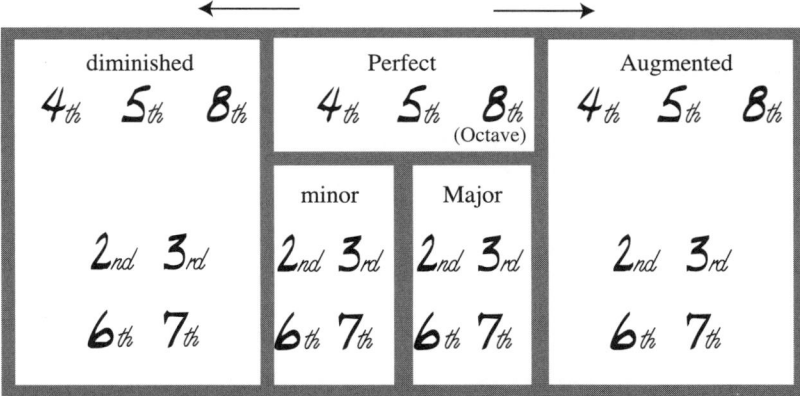

When writing the quality of intervals, lower and upper case letters are important:

Major = M   **Perfect = P**   **minor = m**   **diminished = d**   **Augmented = A**

Review: *steps to identify intervals other than M and P*

1. Count the letter names of the interval notes and all the notes in between:

    F G A B C D E♭ = 7 letters;
    F up to E♭ is a 7th of some kind

2. Call F the "tonic," go up the F major scale and stop on scale degree 7 (E).

3. Questions to ask yourself:

    What is the interval from F–E?   Answer: M7
    Is F–E♭ smaller or larger than F–E?   Answer: smaller
    How much smaller?   Answer: one half step
    Identify F–E♭.   Answer: m7

- *Always* work with letter names first when identifying intervals.
    Look at the keyboard as you identify this interval.
- If you see the note E instead of F♭ you may get the incorrect answer.

The same piano key is played for both of these notes because they are

   harmonic _____   enharmonic _____.

- If you count the letter names first—C D E F—to get a total of four letters,
    you will know C–F♭ is a 4th of some kind and you will avoid making a mistake.

    Identify the interval C–F♭ :_____   Identify the interval C–E:_____

Worksheet

Intervals are altered by making them one half step smaller or larger:
Identify the first interval in each pair. Then change the top note of the second interval in each pair to make it smaller. Identify the new quality of the second interval.

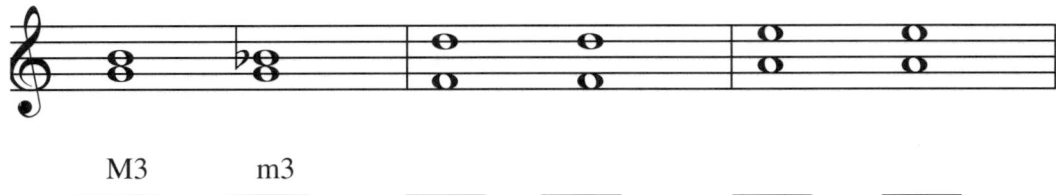

M3   m3

Identify the following intervals:

Is the top note of an interval always used to change its size?

- No. You can also make an interval smaller by raising the lower note; for example:

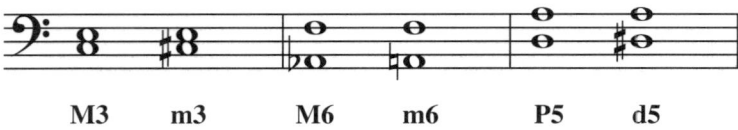

M3   m3   M6   m6   P5   d5

To raise a note (which has no symbol) two half steps, use the symbol (𝄪), a double sharp. Study the major, minor and diminished 6ths below and then write the minor and diminished 7ths by raising the lower note. Play each one.

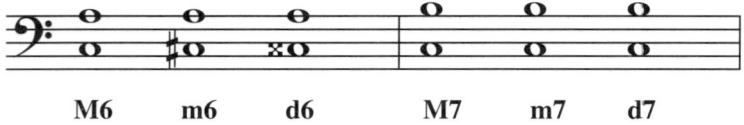

M6   m6   d6   M7   m7   d7

Study the perfect and diminished 4ths below and then write the diminished 5th and diminished octave by raising the lower note of each interval. Play each one.

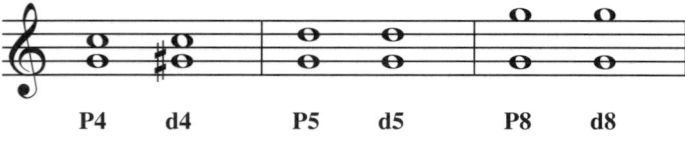

P4   d4   P5   d5   P8   d8

Inverting intervals

To **invert** means to "turn over."
Here is an example of a 3rd and an inverted 3rd:

What interval occurs when a 3rd is inverted? ____

You can invert the 6th to get the original 3rd:

Here is an example of a 2nd and an inverted 2nd:

What interval occurs when a 2nd is inverted? ____

Write the inverted 7th and then invert to get the original 2nd.

Worksheet

Invert these major intervals and identify the quality of the inverted intervals:

M3 ____   M6 ____   M2 ____

As you see, the inverted major interval becomes minor and vice versa:
inverted M = m
inverted m = M

Another reason perfect intervals are called perfect

Review: Perfect intervals are called perfect because they can never become major or minor. To understand another reason, invert some perfect intervals and identify the quality of the inverted intervals:

P4 ____   P5 ____   P4 ____   P5 ____

- When a perfect interval is inverted,

  the quality does ___ does not ___ change.

  Inverted P = P

Worksheet

Make the second interval larger by raising ___ lowering ___ the top note:

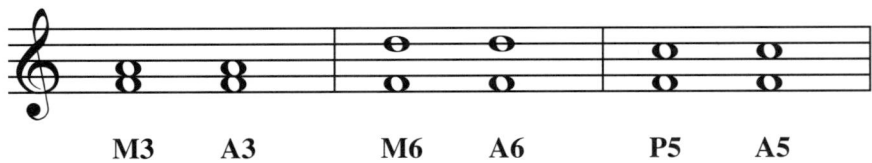

M3   A3   M6   A6   P5   A5

Make the second interval smaller by raising ___ lowering ___ the bottom note:

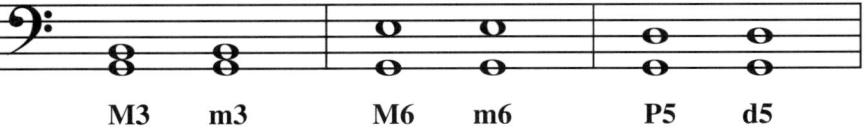

M3   m3   M6   m6   P5   d5

Quiz

1. Identify the quality of the 3rds in this example.

___   ___   ___   ___   ___   ___   ___

Kabalevsky Sonatina in A Minor, Op. 27, No. 18, *LH, meas. 35–39*

2. Identify the quality of the intervals in this example.

Barvinsky The Mouse and the Bear, *LH, meas. 18–end, p. 22*

3. Identify the quality of the intervals in this example.

___   ___

Pease At the Popcorn Ball, *RH, meas. 20, p. 24*

4. Identify the quality of the following intervals.
   Then, write the inversion of each interval
   and identify the quality of each inverted interval.

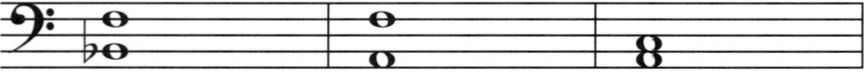

___   ___   ___   ___   ___   ___

Sight reading

1. Identify the RH eighth-note intervals in meas. 1–4.
   Identify the LH eighth-note intervals in meas. 4–7.

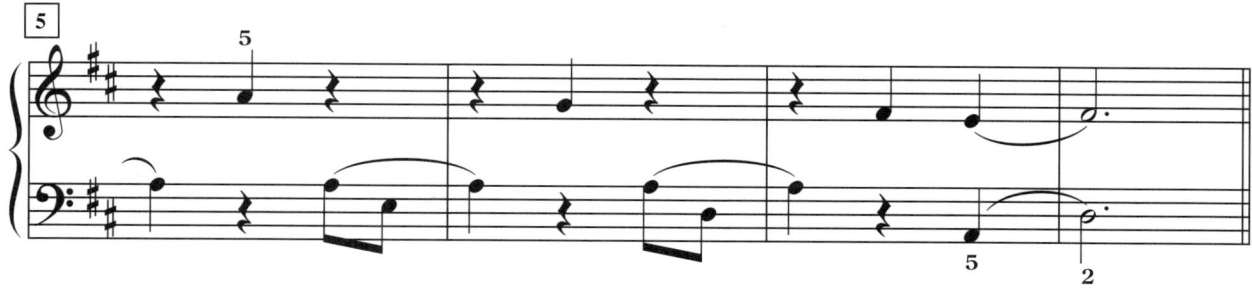

2. In meas. 6, the RH plays a triad with fingers 3 2 1.

   *Name the triad:*_____

   In meas. 1–4, the LH has a common tone of ____.

   Does the LH have any common tones in meas. 5–8? *yes*____ *no*____

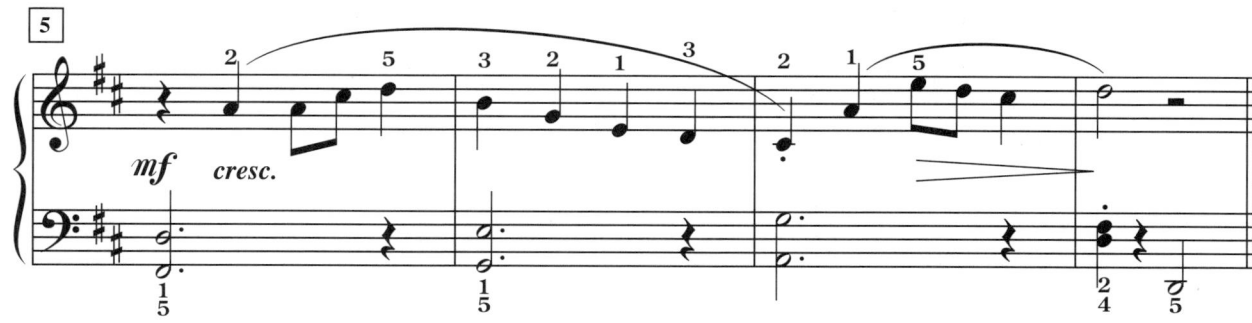

Ear training

Your teacher will play intervals; identify each interval, such as M3.
Now, your teacher will tell you the starting note.
Play the interval you heard, and then invert it.
Say the quality of the inverted interval.
Write each interval and its inversion; use either clef.

Teacher: *Play melodic intervals; play only M, m and P intervals using C, F or G as the starting note.*

Project: *a strange white-key fifth*

In a previous project in the *First Impressions Theory* books, you found one spot on the keyboard where a P5 does not occur between two white keys.

To review that project, play and write a major five-finger pattern starting on B followed by a P5 starting on B (review the whole-half step pattern in the major scale to find the five-finger pattern):

five-finger pattern   *P5*

Now, play and write a major five-finger pattern starting on B♭ followed by a P5 starting on B♭:

five-finger pattern   *P5*

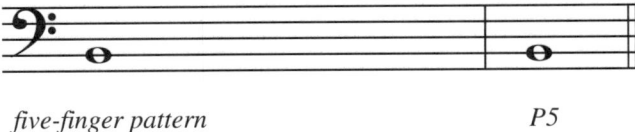

B up to F is a: P5 ____ narrower than a P5 ____
Identify the quality of B up to F: _____ fifth.

B up to F is the only place on the piano where the 5th between two white keys is narrower than a P5. To find the reason for this interesting phenomenon, look on the keyboard below and put an (X) on the white keys where a half step occurs:

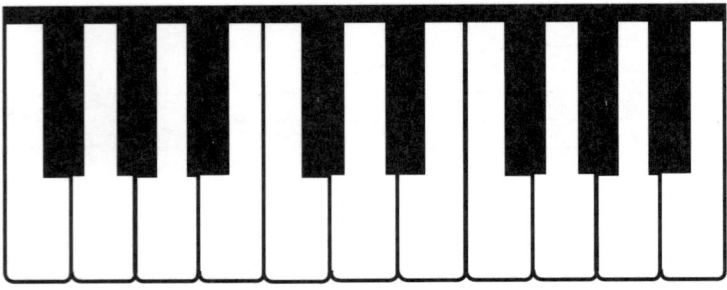

White-key half steps occur between E and ___ , as well as between ___ and ___ .

Do both of those white-key half steps occur between B up to F? yes ___ no ___

If you answered "yes," you know why B up to F is the only white-key diminished 5th.
• A P5 using the letters B and F is only possible by lowering B to B♭, or raising F to F♯.

CHAPTER V
Chords: V7

Review

- You have learned about three triad qualities:

  major   a P5 and M3 above a root
  minor   a P5 and m3 above a root
  diminished a d5 and m3 above a root

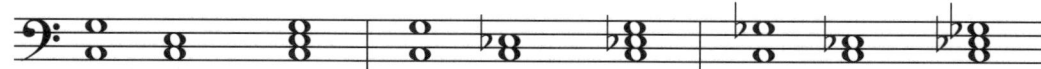

P5 + M3 = Major triad   P5 + m3 = minor triad   d5 + m3 = diminished triad

- Triads can be built on each scale degree (only triads in major keys have been learned).

Upper case is major and lower case is minor; lower case with small circle is diminished.
Primary triads are: **I** (tonic), **IV** (subdominant), **V** (dominant).
Secondary triads are: **ii, iii, vi, vii°**.
Write the Roman numerals under these triads:

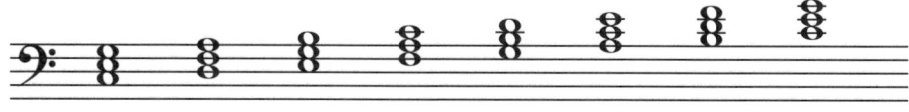

___ ___ ___ ___ ___ ___ ___

- Triads can be written in root position, first inversion or second inversion:

  in root position, the root is the lowest note
  in first inversion, the third is the lowest note
  in second inversion, the fifth is the lowest note

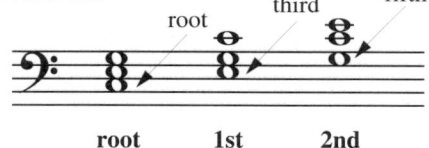

root   1st   2nd

- Triads occur in progressions as seen in the example below.

  The IV is in first ___ second ___ inversion; the V is in first ___ second ___ inversion:

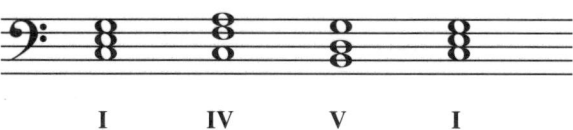

I   IV   V   I

- Cadences occur at the end of sections, phrases and pieces.

Name the Roman numerals and the cadence:

half cadence: ends with V
authentic cadence: V I

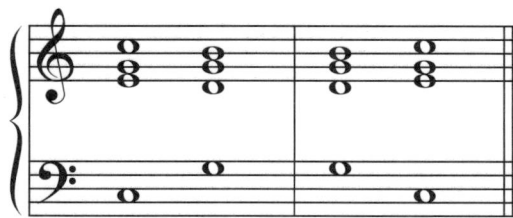

Key of C: I   V   V   I
           Half   Authentic

Spindler Sonatina, Op. 157, No. 4, 2nd movt. meas. 35–36

Key of C :

Roman numerals: ____ ____

Cadence: _____

An enriched chord

Review:

What is the interval from one staff line to the next? 2nd____ 3rd____
What is the interval from one staff space to the next? _____

- In root position, chords are either all line notes or all space notes.

These theory books have presented chords with only three notes; they can be called triads or chords. Another note can be added to a triad to enrich the sound and create a four-note chord.

The most common enriched chord is the one built on the fifth scale degree— the dominant (V) chord:

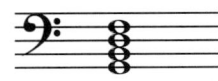

the enriched V in the key of C major

The easiest way to see the enrichment is the addition of another 3rd to a root position V chord. Also identify intervals above the root to fully understand the chord structure. Review: a major triad is a P5 + M3 above a root.

Identify the interval (including the quality) between the root of the enriched V chord and the added note (G–F):

interval, including quality: ____

- The quality of this new four-note chord is called V⁷ or dominant 7th.

The lower three notes are the V chord in C major and the added note creates a m7 above the root.

- The definition for a V⁷: major triad + a m7 above a root.

The 7 in V⁷ refers to the seventh above the root.

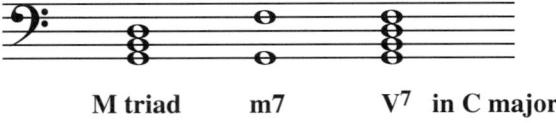

M triad   m7   V⁷ in C major

Musical experiment

Follow these steps to write the V⁷ chord in another key. On the staff below,

1. Write the key signature for G major.
2. Write the V triad in the key of G major.
3. Add the extra third to create a seventh above the root.

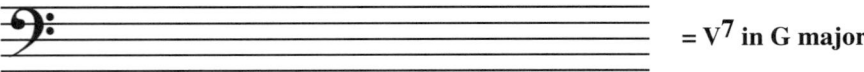 = V⁷ in G major

Is the key signature note used in this V7? yes ___ no ___

Is the V⁷ in harmonic minor keys different from V⁷ in major keys?

When chords are written in a minor key, the harmonic minor form is usually used.
Below, two octaves of the A harmonic minor scale are written.
Circle the notes that form the root position V⁷ and write the chord where indicated:

V⁷ in A minor

Play the V⁷ one note at a time and sing the notes.
Review the quality of the V⁷:

The triad, E G♯ B, is minor ___ major ___ .
The seventh from E up to D is minor ___ major ___ .

• The V⁷ is the same quality in both major and harmonic minor.

The V⁷ in inversions

Since the V⁷ chord has four notes, there is one more possibility
for inverting than is available when inverting triads (three-note chords).
The V⁷ in C major in all its positions is shown here; play each chord:

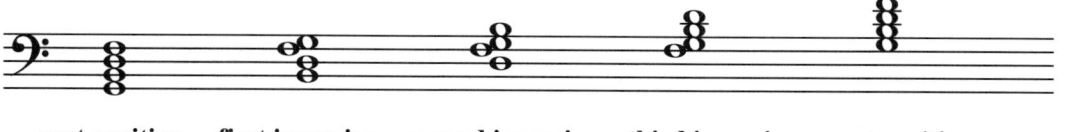

root position   first inversion   second inversion   third inversion   root position

In third inversion, the root____ third____ fifth____ seventh____ is the lowest note.

Worksheet: V⁷ chords in other keys

Using accidentals, write two octaves of the F major scale and then write the V⁷ in F major.

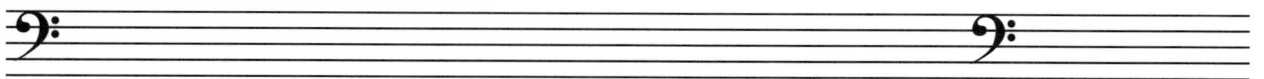

V⁷ in F major

A musical example using V⁷ in E minor is shown below; block the circled notes:

Minuet, from Anna Magdalena Bach's Notebook, *meas. 17–18, p. 4*
Play all of the V⁷ chords in this chapter and listen closely to the sound of each one.
• V⁷'s will be on your ear training.

What if chord tones are spread apart?

Even if the notes of a chord are spread apart, the lowest note still tells the chord's position.
Find the root of an inverted chord by arranging the letter names in thirds; the lowest note is the root.
To know the Roman numeral, the key must be identified first. Answers are supplied for the Gurlitt example; answer the questions for the Spindler example.

Key: _G_
Letter names of circled chord:
(D) F♯ A C .
Circle root. Identify chord. _V7_

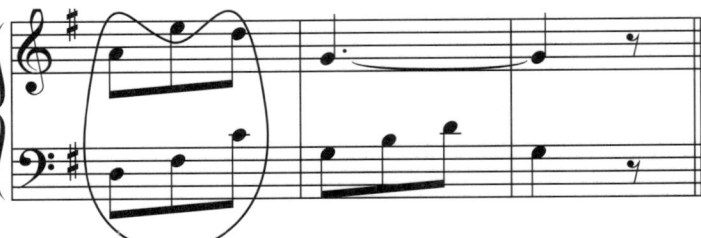

Gurlitt Song Without Words, *meas. 46–48, p. 14*

Key: ___
Letter names of circled chord:
_____

Circle root. Identify chord. ____

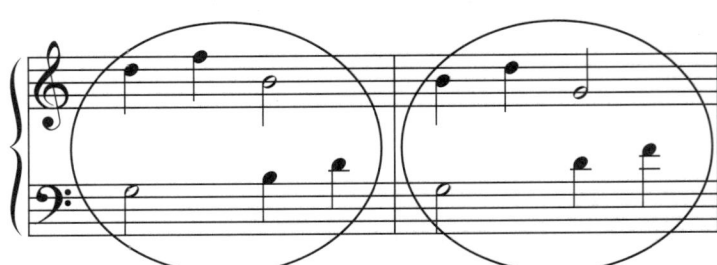

Spindler Sonatina, Op. 147, No. 4, *1st movt., meas. 18–19, p. 11*

Worksheet

Follow these steps to analyze the V7 chord circled below:

1. Write the four letter names of the chord; play all the notes: ___ ___ ___ ___
2. Arrange and write the letters in thirds: _____
3. Circle the root in the letters and in the music.
4. Identify the position of the chord: _____

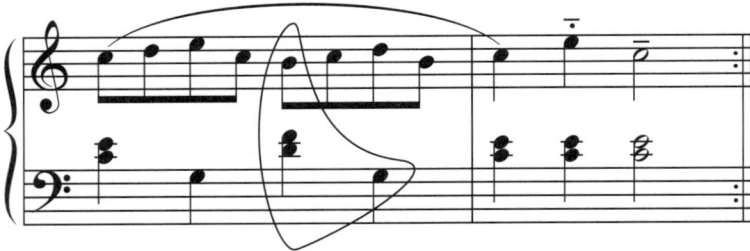

Spindler Sonatina, Op. 157, No. 4, *1st movt., meas. 7–8, p. 10*

Ear training

Your teacher will give you the name of the starting note and then play some melodic and haromonic triads in root position or one of the inversions. Sing the notes of each chord and play what your teacher played.

Name the root, quality and position of each chord.

1. root and quality ____ position ____
2. root and quality ____ position ____
3. root and quality ____ position ____
4. root and quality ____ position ____

Teacher: *Play major or minor chords in root position or inversions.*
Play in the student's vocal range and play melodically, then harmonically.

You will hear two four-note chords. Identify which one has the V7 quality.

Teacher: *Major seventh and V7 chords or half-diminished seventh and V7 chords make good sets.*
Play the chords melodically, then harmonically.

Quiz

1. Write the root position V7 in the keys of G major and F major; write symbols as accidentals:

   V7 in G major   V7 in F major

2. In the key of G, write the V7 and all its inversions:

   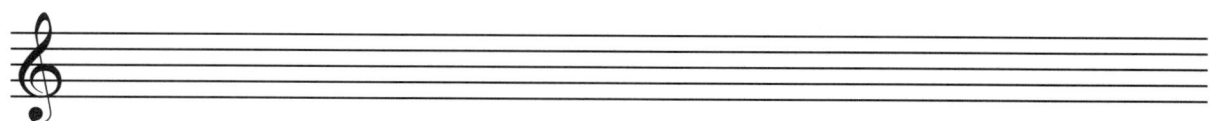

3. Identify the intervals above the root of the root position V7 chord; the first is given:

   __M3__   _____   _____

4. Identify the inversion of each chord:

   ____   ____   ____   ____

5. Identify the root, quality and inversion of the circled chords. Use R for root; use 1st or 2nd for first or second inversion.

   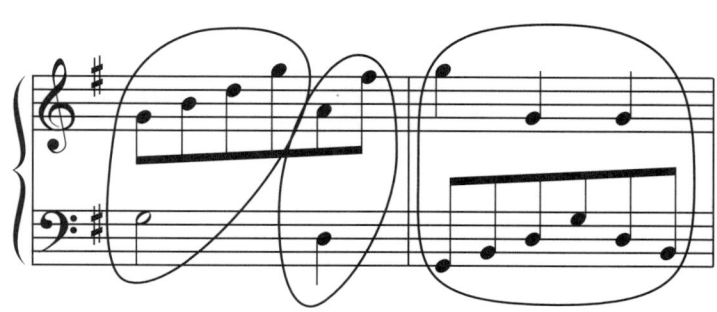

   Minuet, from Anna Magdalena Bach's Notebook, *meas. 1–3, p. 4*

   Key: _____ Meas. 1 _____ _____ Meas. 2 _____

Sight reading

1. Study the RH intervals in meas. 1–4. Then, study the LH intervals in meas. 5–6.

2. Compare the RH patterns in meas. 1–4 with the LH patterns in meas. 5–7.

Project: *learning more about the V⁷*

A short piece in C major is written below. In one measure, the V⁷ chord occurs.
Begin your project by identifying each LH chord with a Roman numeral.
Play the whole piece.

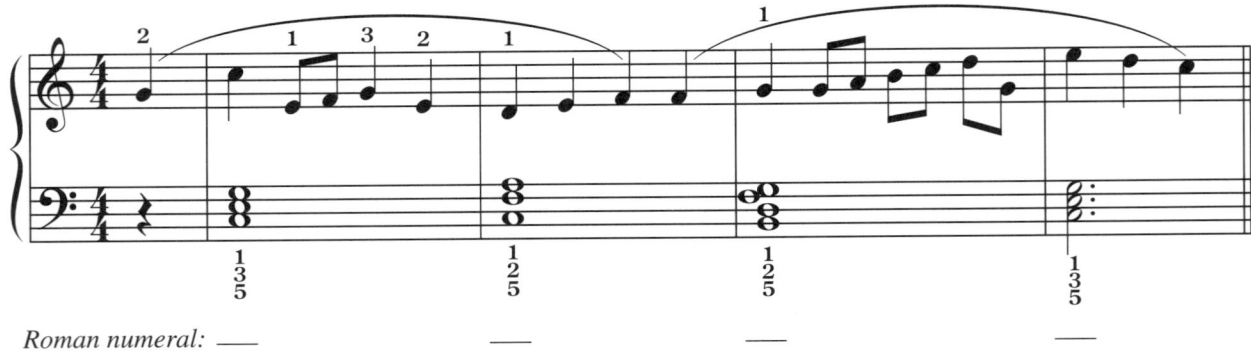

Roman numeral: ___   ___   ___   ___

1. Circle all scale degrees 3 and 6 in both hands; they may occur more than once.

2. Copy the piece below and lower scale degrees 3 and 6
   to make the C harmonic minor sound.

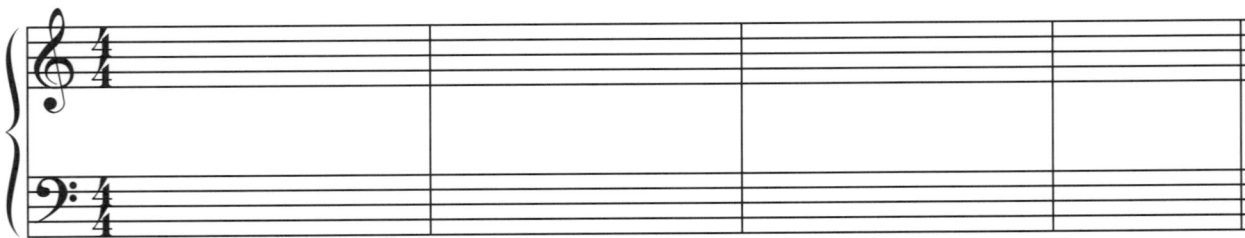

Are C major and C minor relative___or parallel ___?

- The V7 is the same quality in both major and harmonic minor:

    true ____ *false* ____

CHAPTER VI
Phrases and Period;
Nonharmonic Tones; Dissonance/Resolution

Phrases

In spoken language, words are grouped in phrases to form parts of sentences.
In the same way, measures in music are grouped to form **phrases**:

Spindler Sonatina, Op. 157, No. 4,
2nd movt., meas. 1–2, p. 12

Question and answer phrases

When someone asks you a question, you give an answer that directly relates to the question.
Two adjacent musical phrases that complement one another are called **question-and-answer phrases:**

Spindler Sonatina, Op. 157, No. 4, 2nd movt., meas. 1–4, p. 12

Period

A section of music with at least two question-and-answer phrases is called a **period.**
The word "period" refers to an interval of time. The above example (meas. 1–4) is a period.

Cadences

In language, a dot is written to indicate the end of a sentence.
In music, a cadence indicates the end of a phrase or period. Sometimes the cadence is incomplete, as in a half cadence, and sometimes the cadence is more complete, as in an authentic cadence.
In meas. 4, the last chord is V, a half cadence. In meas. 8 on page 34, the LH plays the root of V and root of I, representing those chords which form *a half ___ authentic ___ cadence.*

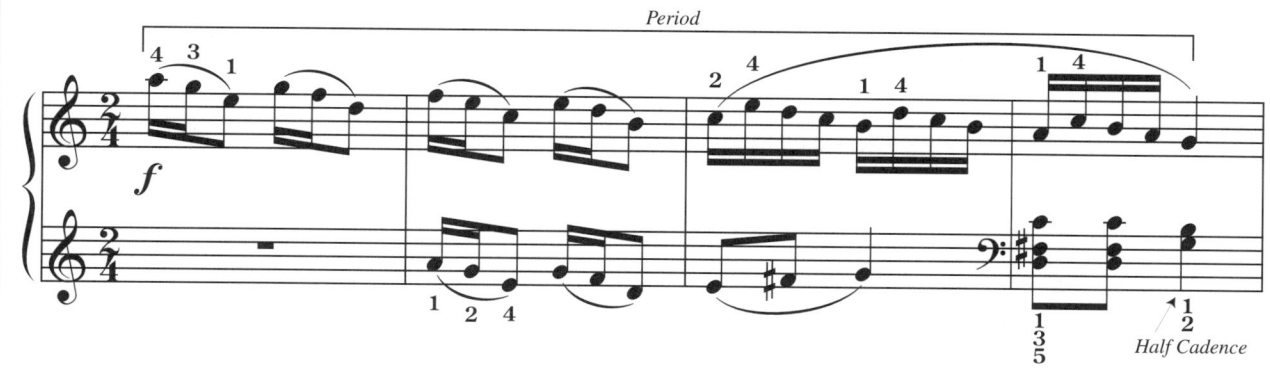

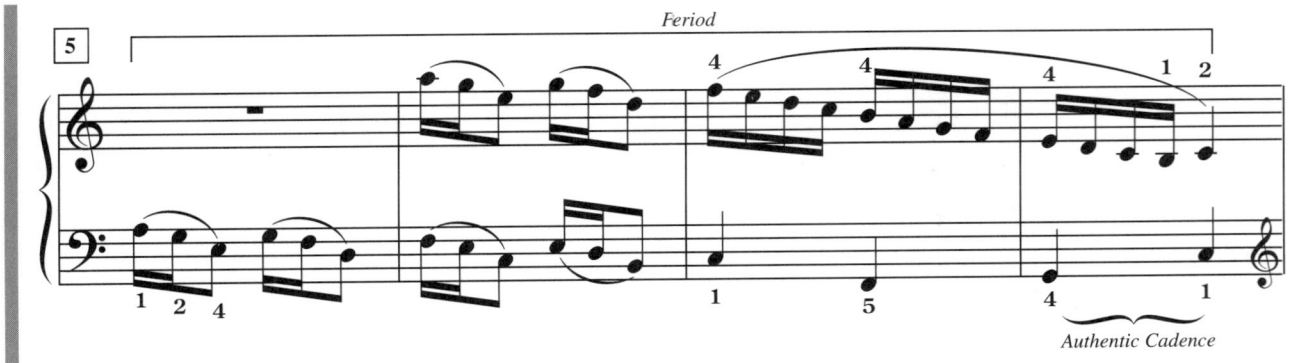

Spindler Sonatina, Op. 157, No. 4, *2nd movt., meas. 1–8, p. 12*

Harmonic and nonharmonic notes or tones

Harmony refers to chords and chord progressions.
Chords accompanying a melody use some of the melody notes to create a blended sound.
The melody notes that match chord tones are called **harmonic notes** or **tones.**

To create variety, melodies also use notes *not* contained in the chords. These notes are called **nonharmonic notes** or **tones.**

Neighbor tones

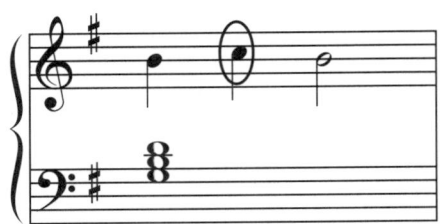

A common nonharmonic tone is a **neighbor tone.** For this example, write the letter names of the LH chord and the letter name of the circled note. You will see that the circled note is a nonharmonic tone and the other notes are harmonic tones.

*Chord letter names*____

*RH circled note*____

When you visit your neighbor, you eventually return home. Neighbor tones return to their original pitch. Neighbor tones can be upper or lower neighbors. The above example shows an upper neighbor tone. The following examples show both upper and lower neighbor tones:

C major   G major   G major   C minor

Spindler Sonatina, Op. 157, No. 4, *1st movt., meas. 1–2 and meas. 9–10*

Passing tones

A nonharmonic tone that occurs between two chord tones is called a **passing tone.** In the example:

1. Identify the key.
2. Write in the letter names for each circled chord.
3. Write the letter name for each RH circled note.

By doing these three steps, you will see why the circled RH notes are called passing tones.

RH circled notes: ____ ____

Key: ____

Chord letter names: _____ _____ _____

Spindler Sonatina, Op. 157, No. 4,
1st movt., meas. 7–8

Appoggiatura

The word "appoggiatura" comes from an Italian word that means "to lean on."
An **appoggiatura** is a nonharmonic tone that is a step above or below a chord tone.
It is usually stressed to create the feeling of leaning on the note:

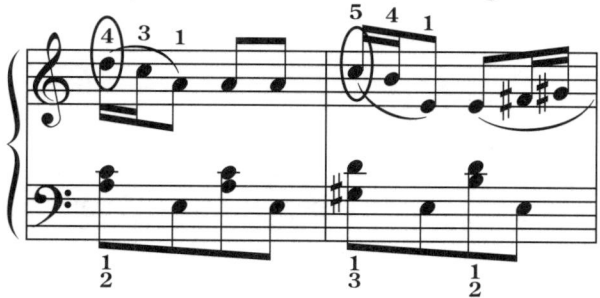

Spindler Sonatina, Op. 157, No. 4, *2nd movt., meas. 42–43, p. 13*

The example below shows two simultaneous appoggiaturas in the RH, on C and E.
This is an example of a double appoggiatura.

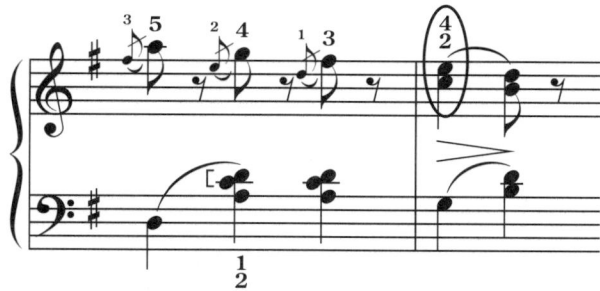

Kullak Dance on the Lawn, *meas. 3–4, p. 15*

Dissonance and resolution

A dissonance is a sound that clashes or does not blend with the other notes around it. Nonharmonic tones are **dissonant.** Play this example which uses notes from meas. 7 of the Spindler *Sonatina* illustrated at the bottom of the previous page:

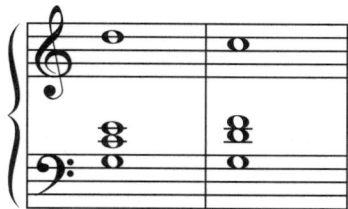

When the nonharmonic tone returns to a harmonic tone, the dissonance is neutralized, resulting in a **resolution**.

In music, dissonance creates exciting moments; it is similar to adding spice to food.
The spice may sting your tongue, but a cool drink of water resolves the stinging!

Play all of the nonharmonic examples in this chapter.
If you stop on each nonharmonic note and play the chord with it, you will hear that the note is dissonant.

Play the chord again with the resolution tone to hear that the dissonance is neutralized.

Identifying nonharmonic tones in your music

Use these abbreviations when identifying nonharmonic tones in your music:

UNT = upper neighbor tone
LNT = lower neighbor tone
PT = passing tone
App = appoggiatura

Quiz

1. Identify the LH chord and then identify the RH nonharmonic tone:

   Gurlitt Song without Words, *meas. 10, p. 14*

   Root and quality of LH chord: _____   *RH neighbor tone:* ____ *passing tone:* ____

2. The circle shows three notes in a V⁷ chord. Write the letter names you see in the circle, and then identify the type of nonharmonic tone in the RH (the note C):

   Letter names of the V⁷ chord: _____
   Type of nonharmonic tone in RH: _____

Pease At the Popcorn Ball, *meas. 15, p. 23*

Ear training

Your teacher will play one of the measures in each set. Name which measure you heard and then identify the nonharmonic tone.

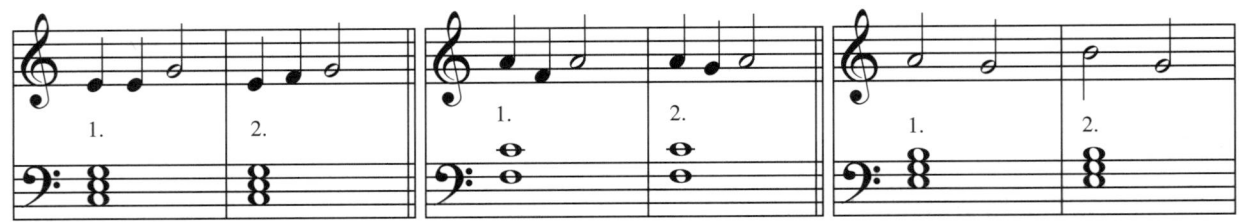

Teacher: *In each set play the measure with the nonharmonic tone.*

Project: *reading the secret code of the missing notes*

In this example, you can see abbreviations for various nonharmonic tones (refer to the chart of abbreviations on the previous page). Write in the nonharmonic tone in the circle. When you are done, play the piece as a sight-reading example. The comma in meas. 2 and meas. 4 means to break the sound between phrases.

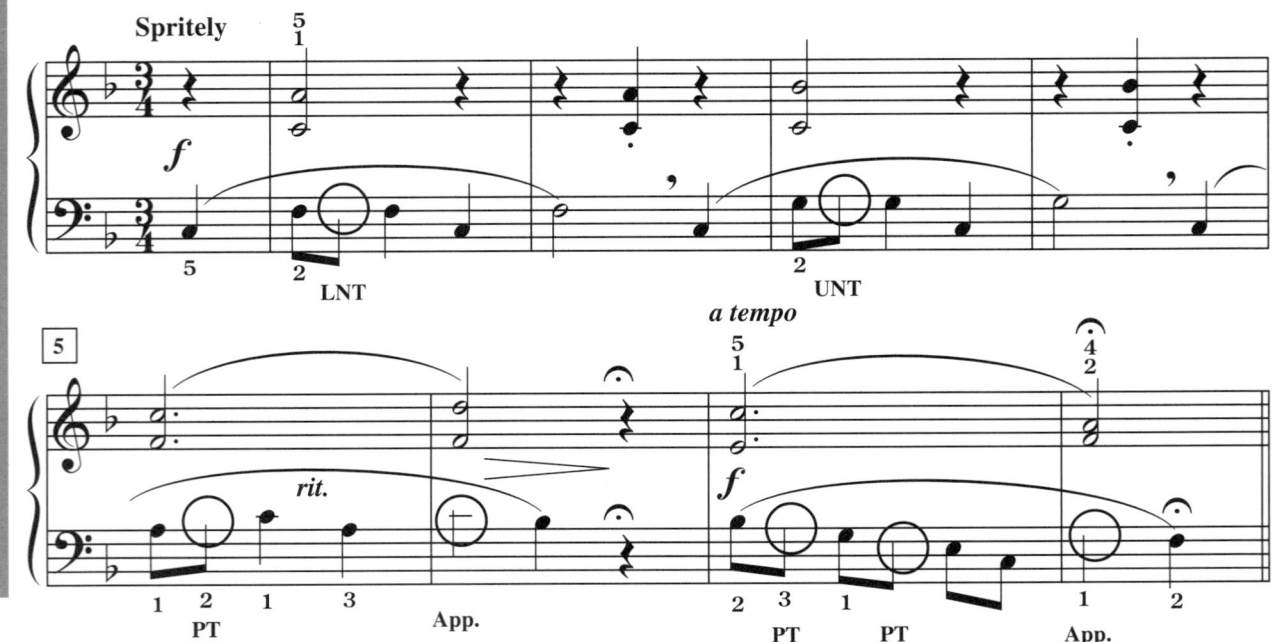

GLOSSARY

Appoggiatura: a nonharmonic tone that is a step above or below a harmonic tone (p. 35). See **Nonharmonic tones, Neighbor tone** and **Passing tone**.

Augment: to make larger (Vol. 1). See **Diminish**.

Authentic cadence: a cadence formed with V–I (i) (Vol. 1). See **Half cadence**.

Cadence: a stopping place; cadences are usually formed with chords (Vol. 1). See **Authentic cadence** and **Half cadence**.

Chord progression: a succession of chords such as I–IV–V–I (Vol. 1).

Cycle of fifths: a circle around which the major and minor keys are arranged. The word cycle refers to regularly repeating patterns that occur between the keys (p. 11).

Diminish: to make smaller (Vol. 1). See **Augment**.

Dissonance: a sound that clashes or does not blend with the other notes around it (p. 35). See **Resolution**.

Dominant: the fifth note of a scale. A chord built on that note is called the dominant chord (p. 10). See **Tonic** and **Subdominant**.

Dominant seventh chord: a M3, P5 and m7 above the fifth scale degree of a major or harmonic minor scale (p. 28).

Double flat or sharp: the symbol (♭♭) or (𝄪); respectively lowers or raises a note two half steps (Vol. 1).

First inversion: a chord that has its third as the lowest note (Vol. 1). See **Inverted chord**.

Half cadence: a cadence that ends with the V chord (Vol. 1). See **Authentic cadence**.

Harmonic minor form: one of the three minor forms. The seventh scale degree of the natural minor is raised (Vol. 1). See **Melodic minor form** and **Natural minor form**.

Imitation: musical material repeated in another hand or another voice (Vol. 1). See **Repetition** and **Sequence**.

Inverted chord: a chord that does not have the root as the lowest note (Vol. 1). See **First inversion, Second inversion, Third inversion** and **Root position**.

Inverted interval: an interval that has the lower note moved up an octave to become the higher note, or the upper note moved down to become the lower note (p. 23).

Melodic minor form: one of the three minor forms. Ascending, degrees 6 and 7 of the natural minor form are raised; descending, degrees 6 and 7 are returned to the notes of the natural minor form (Vol. 1). See **Harmonic minor form** and **Natural minor form**.

Meter: the number of big beats in a measure; duple meter has two big beats (such as 2/4 or 6/8), triple meter (such as 3/4) has three big beats, etc. (p. 3).

Natural minor form: the form of the minor scale that has no altered notes; a natural minor scale uses the same notes as the relative major scale (Vol. 1). See **Melodic minor form** and **Harmonic minor form**.

Neighbor tone: a note just above or below a harmonic tone; an upper neighbor tone is above and a lower neighbor tone is below (p. 34). See **Appoggiatura, Nonharmonic tones** and **Passing tone**.

Nonharmonic tones: notes not part of the harmony (chord); common nonharmonic tones are passing tones, plus upper and lower neighbor tones (p. 34). See **Appoggiatura, Neighbor tone** and **Passing tone**.

Ostinato: a recurring pattern, often in the bass (Vol. 1).

Parallel major and minor: a major scale and a minor scale that share the same tonic note. C major and C minor are parallel major and minor scales (p. 17). See **Relative major and minor**.

Passing tone: a nonharmonic tone that moves between two chord tones; for instance, in a C major triad, D played after C and moving to E is a passing tone (p. 34). See **Appoggiatura, Neighbor tones** and **Nonharmonic tones**.

Pedal tone: a note sustained or repeated while harmonies change; a pedal tone is usually in the bass (Vol. 1).

Period: two or more phrases (p. 33). See **Phrase**.

Phrase: a short section of music that is like a clause in language; two or more phrases make a period which is more complete than a phrase (p. 33). See **Period**.

Primary triads: triads built on scale degrees 1, 4 and 5 (Vol. 1). See **Secondary triads**.

Relative major and minor: major and minor scales that share the same key signature. C major and A minor are relative major and minor scales (Vol. 1). See **Parallel major and minor**.

Repetition: repeated musical material (Vol. 1). See **Imitation** and **Sequence**.

Resolution: a dissonance is neutralized, as when a nonharmonic tone returns to a harmonic tone (p. 35). See **Dissonance**.

Rhythmic motive: a short rhythmic unit that is used often in a composition (p. 5).

Root position: a chord that has the root as the lowest note (Vol. 1). See **Inverted chord**.

Second inversion: a chord that has its fifth as the lowest note (Vol. 1). See **Inverted chord**.

Secondary triads: triads built on scale degrees 2, 3, 6 and 7 (Vol. 1). See **Primary triads**.

Sequence: musical material repeated a little higher or lower (Vol. 1). See **Imitation** and **Repetition**.

Seventh chord: a four-note chord that consists of a third, fifth and seventh above the root (p. 28). See **Dominant seventh chord**.

Subdominant: the fourth note of a scale. A chord built on that note is called the subdominant chord (p.10). See **Dominant** and **Tonic**.

Syncopation: an accent on what is usually a weak beat of the measure (p. 7).

Third inversion: a chord that has its seventh as the lowest note (p. 29). See **Inverted chord**.

Tonic: the first note of a scale. A chord built on that note is called the tonic chord (p.10). See **Dominant** and **Subdominant**.

Some musical character words and their definitions:

animato	animated; lively
cantabile	in a singing style
dolce	sweetly
espressivo	expressively
leggiero	lightly
spiritoso	spirited

QUIZ

1. In this example, the upbeats are circled.
   Write in the count of the measure where each upbeat occurs.

2. Finish writing the counts for this example.

             &   1 &

3. What is the meter of $\frac{6}{8}$? triple ___ duple ___ .

4. Draw 2 notes to equal each of these notes.

   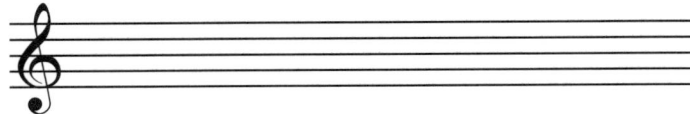

5. Write the lower tetrachord of the E♭ major scale.

   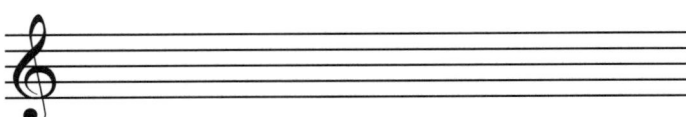

6. Write the upper tetrachord of the G major scale.

7. In what major key is this example?

   March, from Anna Magdalena Bach's Notebook, meas. 1–2, p. 6

8. Write sharp symbols to create the A major scale.

   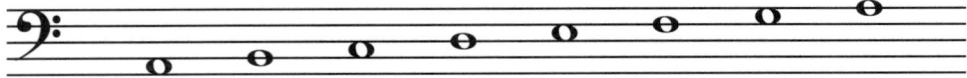

9. Identify the following major key signatures:

10. Write symbols to create the C melodic minor scale:

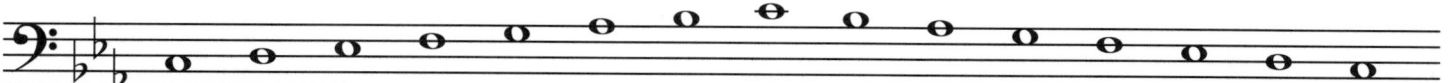

11. What is the relative minor of G major? _____

12. Identify the quality (such as M3 or P5) of these intervals:

___ ___ ___ ___ ___

13. Identify the quality of this interval. Then, write the interval in inversion and identify the inverted interval.

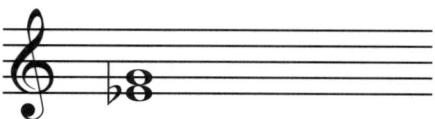

___ ___

14. First, identify the major keys of each key signature. Then write the notes for the V7 chord in each key:

key:____   key:____   key:____   key:____

15. Name the root of these inverted V⁷ chords. Then, name the major key in which each V⁷ occurs.

root: ____ ____ ____

key: ____ ____ ____

16. These are initials for some nonharmonic tones. Write the words for each one:

UNT _____ **LNT** _____

PT _____

17. First, identify the circled chords in the LH.

Then, identify the circled nonharmonic tones in the RH by using the initials.

NH tone: ____   ____   ____   ____

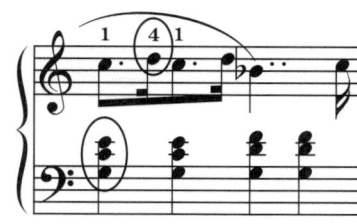

chord: ____   ____   ____   ____

Spindler Sonatina, Op. 157, No. 4,   *Kabalevsky* Sonatina in A Minor,   *Kabalevsky* Sonatina in A Minor,
2nd movt., meas. 42–44, p. 13   Op. 27, meas. 17, p. 20   Op. 27, meas. 6, p. 20

18. Which is shorter? *a period* ___ *a phrase* ___ .

SIGHT READING

Questions about your sight reading piece:

19. *The major key of two sharps is _____ .*

The minor key of two sharps is _____ .

Is this piece in major ___ or minor ___ ?

20. In the LH part, how many A♯'s do you find?

3___ 4___ 5___ .

Are there any A♯'s in the RH part? yes ___ no ___

21. In meas. 9–10, the RH plays on small beats

number ____ and number ____ .

In meas. 15–16, the LH plays on small beats

number ____ and number ____ .

22. Between meas. 11–12,

is the RH tied ___ or slurred ___ ?

In meas. 18,

is the LH A♯ tied ___ or slurred ___ ?

Sad Farewell

Alan Oettinger

ERRATA

p. 11   text paragraph one: James Montgomery, not Mongomery.
p. 24   top picture caption: H. M. King Hussein in center, not H. R. H. Hussein.
pp. 53 and 108 picture captions: Anne Ogilvy, not Ann Ogilvy.
p. 74   1997 awards list: Carolyn Draper Rivers, not Draper-Rivers.
p. 86   picture caption number 7: Ernest Frerichs, not Frericks.
p. 98   bottom picture caption: Martha Joukowsky, not Joukowski.
p. 108 Class of 2003 picture caption: Robert D. Miller II, not MIller II.
p. 108 Class of 2003 picture caption and passim: Øystein La Bianca, not Oystein.
p. 109 Honorary Trustees picture caption: C.C. Lamberg-Karlovsky, not C.C. Lamberg.
p. 109 Honorary Trustees picture caption: Elizabeth Moynihan, not Liz Moynahan.
p. 114 Fellowships offered list: Nies Fellow in Mesopotamian Civilization, not Neis Fellow.
p. 143 first picture caption: G. R. H. "Mick" Wright, not G. H. R.
pp. 143 and 268 first picture captions: Roger Boraas, not Borass.
p. 248 bottom picture caption: Denyse Homes-Fredericq of Belgium, not Belgiun.
p. 289 text paragraph: Finnish scholars, not Finish.
p. 292 top picture caption: Queen Sofia, not Sopia.
p. 294 right picture caption: at left is Jim Fisher, not Penny Clifford.